Name _____

Working at Age Eight?

 Investigate

1. What is happening in this photograph?

_____

_____

2. What did you notice first about the photograph? Why?

_____

_____

 Question

3. After studying this photograph, what do you want to learn more about? How will you find out?

_____

_____

4. What countries still allow underage children to work? If you don't know, look in books and on safe Internet sites to find out.

_____

_____

 Understand

5. Based on this text and what you see in the photograph, do you think child labor laws are a good idea? Explain.

_____

_____

6. Imagine working in an oyster factory in 1911. Describe how your life would be different.

_____

_____

To Buy or Not to Buy?

If you go to New York City, you will probably see street vendors. They set up their carts on almost any corner. They sell things to the public. One hundred years ago, they did the same thing.

People who came to the United States from other places might arrive in New York. Many moved to other parts of the country. A large number of people from Italy stayed in New York. They would live near others from their hometowns back in Italy. This neighborhood was called Little Italy. Many of them spoke the same language. Some even knew each other from Italy!

These neighbors would celebrate weddings, feasts, christenings (baby baptisms), and funerals together. They would hold *festas,* or parades. The parades would celebrate saints. Street vendors would line the streets and sell lots of items.

This photograph was taken during a festival in Little Italy during 1908. Look at all of the things for sale! Does it look like they were having fun?

80-2 STREET VENDER, ITALIAN FEAST

To Buy or Not to Buy?

If you go to New York City, you will probably see street vendors. They set up their carts on almost any corner and sell things to the public. One hundred years ago, they did the same thing.

People who came to the United States from other places might arrive in New York. Many moved to other parts of the country. A large number of people from Italy stayed in New York. They would live near others from their hometown. This neighborhood was called Little Italy. Many of them spoke the same language and even knew each other from Italy!

These neighbors would celebrate weddings, feasts, christenings (baby baptisms), and funerals together. They would sometimes hold *festas*, or parades celebrating saints. During these times, street vendors would line the streets and sell lots of items.

This photograph was taken during a festival in Little Italy during 1908. Look at all of the things for sale! Does it look like they were having fun?

80-2 STREET VENDER, ITALIAN FEAST

To Buy or Not to Buy?

If you visit New York City, you can expect to see street vendors. They set up their carts on almost any corner and sell items to the public. One century ago, they did the same thing.

People who came to the United States from other countries would often arrive in New York. Many moved to different areas of the country. However, a large number of people from Italy stayed in the city. They would often live near others from their hometown in a neighborhood called Little Italy. Many of them spoke the same language and even knew each other from Italy!

These neighbors would celebrate weddings, feasts, christenings (baby baptisms), and funerals together. They would sometimes hold *festas*, or parades celebrating saints. During these times, street vendors would line the streets and sell lots of items.

This photograph was taken during a festival in Little Italy during 1908. Look at all of the things for sale! Does it look like they were having fun?

80-2 STREET VENDER, ITALIAN FEAST

To Buy or Not to Buy?

🔍 Investigate

1. What is happening in this photograph?

    _____

    _____

2. What did you notice first about the photograph? Why?

    _____

    _____

❓ Question

3. After studying this photograph, what is one question you have? How will you find the answer?

    _____

    _____

4. What types of things do street vendors sell today? If you don't know, look in books and on safe Internet sites to find out.

    _____

    _____

 Understand

5. Based on this text, why do you think people from the same hometown chose to live near each other in the new world?

    _____

    _____

6. Imagine working as a street vendor. Describe how your life would be different.

    _____

    _____

Is the Sky the Limit?

Today, women are able to work in any job and do anything that men are able to. One hundred years ago that was not possible. Women were not considered equal to men at that time in the United States.

Women were able to fight for their country. They could work. They were not able to vote. They were not kept safe by the US Constitution. Many people thought this was not fair. They fought for change. They felt women should have the same rights as men. This fight for change was called women's suffrage.

On August 26, 1920, the Nineteenth Amendment to the Constitution was passed. Women were given the same rights and citizenship as men! That year, women voted in the US elections for the very first time.

This cartoon is from October 1920. It is a print made on a printing press. It is called "The sky is now her limit." It shows a woman holding buckets on a yoke. She is standing at a ladder that is reaching to the sky.

Library of Congress, LC-DIG-ppmsca-02919

Is the Sky the Limit?

Today, women are able to work in any job and achieve anything. One hundred years ago that was not possible. Women were not considered equal to men at that time in the United States.

Women were able to fight for their country. They could work in factories and shops. They were not able to vote. They were not protected by the US Constitution. Many people believed this was unfair and fought for change. This fight for change was called women's suffrage.

On August 26, 1920, the Nineteenth Amendment to the Constitution was approved, or *ratified*. Women were finally given the same rights and responsibilities of citizenship as men! That year, women voted in the US elections for the very first time.

This cartoon is from October 1920. It is a *photomechanical print,* or a print made on a printing press. It is called "The sky is now her limit." It shows a woman holding buckets on a yoke. She is standing at a ladder that is reaching to the sky.

Library of Congress, LC-DIG-ppmsca-02919

Is the Sky the Limit?

Today, women are able to work in any job and achieve anything that men are able to. One hundred years ago that was not possible. Women were not considered equal citizens of the United States.

Women were able to fight for their country and work in factories, but they were not able to vote. They were not protected by the US Constitution. Many people believed this was unfair and fought for change. This fight for change was called women's suffrage.

On August 26, 1920, the Nineteenth Amendment to the Constitution was approved, or *ratified*. Women were finally given the same rights and responsibilities of citizenship as men! That year, women voted in the US elections for the very first time.

This cartoon is from October 1920. It is a *photomechanical print*, or a print made on a printing press. It is called "The sky is now her limit." It shows a woman holding buckets on a yoke. She is standing at a ladder that is reaching to the sky.

Library of Congress, LC-DIG-ppmsca-02919

Is the Sky the Limit?

 Investigate

1. What did you notice first about the cartoon? Why?

   _____

   _____

2. What rungs from the ladder have women achieved today? How do you know?

   _____

   _____

 Question

3. After studying this cartoon, what do you want to learn more about?

   _____

   _____

4. Can all women vote today? Name any places where women cannot vote. If you don't know, look in books and on safe Internet sites to find out.

   _____

   _____

Understand

5. Explain the message behind the cartoon.

   _____

   _____

6. Imagine that your mother was alive in the United States in 1911. Describe how her life would be different.

   _____

   _____

For Sale!

Today, people use advertisements (ads) to sell things. Ads have been around for many, many years. One hundred years ago, people also used ads to sell slaves.

Long ago, buying and selling slaves was seen as a business. Slaves belonged to their owner, just like a car does today. If an owner wanted to sell a slave, he might post an ad. He could also take the slave to an auction. Slave auctions happened downtown.

Many families were split up at these sales. Slaves were usually sold one at a time. A man in good health would sell for $1,000 to $1,500. A woman in good health would sell for $300 to $500. A child would sell for $150 to $200.

The advertisement on this page is not for selling slaves. It was placed by Thomas Griggs, a man willing to buy slaves. He lived in Charleston, South Carolina.

CASH!

All persons that have SLAVES to dispose of, will do well by giving me a call, as I will give the

HIGHEST PRICE FOR

Men, Women, & CHILDREN.

Any person that wishes to sell, will call at Hill's tavern, or at Shannon Hill for me, and any information they want will be promptly attended to.

Thomas Griggs.

Charlestown, May 7, 1835.

PRINTED AT THE FREE PRESS OFFICE, CHARLESTOWN.

For Sale!

Today, people use advertisements (ads) to sell their products. Ads have been around for many, many years. One hundred years ago, people also used ads to sell slaves.

Long ago, the buying and selling of slaves was seen as a business. Slaves were the property of their owner, much like a car or home is today. If an owner wanted to sell a slave, he would either post an ad or take the slave to an auction. Slave auctions happened downtown.

Many families were separated at these sales because slaves were usually sold one at a time. A man in good health would sell for $1,000 to $1,500. A woman in good health would sell for $300 to $500. A child would sell for $150 to $200.

The advertisement on this page is not for selling slaves. It was placed by Thomas Griggs, a man willing to buy slaves. He lived in Charleston, South Carolina.

CASH!

All persons that have **SLAVES** to dispose of, will do well by giving me a call, as I will give the

HIGHEST PRICE FOR

Men, Women, &
CHILDREN.

Any person that wishes to sell, will call at Hill's tavern, or at Shannon Hill for me, and any information they want will be promptly attended to.

Thomas Griggs.

Charlestown, May 7, 1835.

PRINTED AT THE FREE PRESS OFFICE, CHARLESTOWN.

Library of Congress, LC-USZ62-62799

For Sale!

Today, people use advertisements (ads) to sell their products. Ads have been around for many, many years. One hundred years ago, people also used ads to sell slaves.

In the nineteenth century, the buying and selling of slaves was considered a business. Slaves were the property of their owner, much like a car or home is today. If an owner wanted to sell a slave, he would either post an ad or take the slave to an auction. Slave auctions happened downtown.

Many families were separated at these sales because slaves were usually sold one at a time. A man in good health would sell for $1,000 to $1,500; a woman in good health would sell for $300 to $500; and a child would sell for $150 to $200.

The advertisement on this page is not for selling slaves. It was placed by Thomas Griggs, a man willing to buy slaves. He lived in Charleston, South Carolina.

CASH!

All persons that have **SLAVES** to dispose of, will do well by giving me a call, as I will give the

HIGHEST PRICE FOR

Men, Women, &

CHILDREN.

Any person that wishes to sell, will call at **Hill's tavern**, or at **Shannon Hill** for me, and any information they want will be promptly attended to.

Thomas Griggs.

Charlestown, May 7, 1835.

PRINTED AT THE FREE PRESS OFFICE, CHARLESTOWN.

For Sale!

 Investigate

1. What did you notice first about the advertisement? Why?

   _____

   _____

2. Why do you think Mr. Griggs placed this ad? What was he thinking at the time?

   _____

   _____

 Question

3. After studying this advertisement, what do you want to learn more about?

   _____

   _____

4. Do any countries allow slavery today? Look in books and on safe Internet sites to find out. Then, write about what you have learned.

   _____

   _____

 Understand

5. Based on this text and the ad, do you think families were split up? Why or why not?

   _____

   _____

6. Based on the text in this advertisement, do you think an ad like this would be placed today? Why or why not?

   _____

   _____

North versus South

When the United States fought to gain its freedom from England in 1776, the entire country was united. Within just a few decades that all changed. What caused this fight? Slavery.

The people living in the North had smaller farms that used free *labor,* or work. These states used their money for banks and insurance. They built better transportation systems. They also worked hard at improving communication.

The people living in the South had much larger farms called *plantations*. They grew crops like cotton and tobacco. They needed many more workers. They used a lot of their money to buy slaves.

The North and the South did not agree when it came to slavery. They fought every time a new state was added to the United States. The South did not want to give up slavery because that is how it made most of its money. The North did not feel slavery was right.

This map from 1860 shows how the states were divided. This division of states led to the Civil War. The map was printed from a wood engraving.

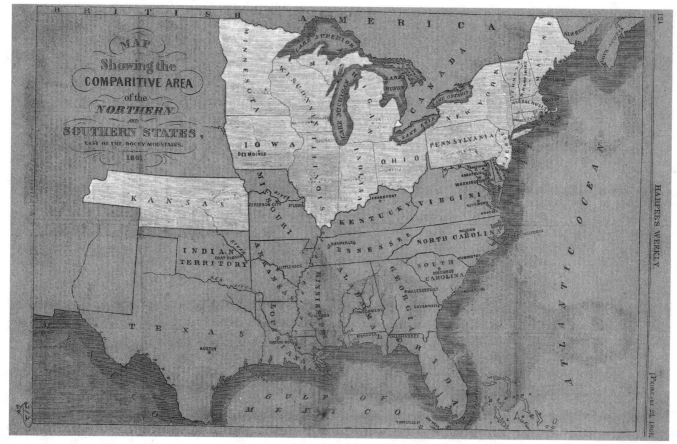

North versus South

When the United States fought to gain its freedom from England in 1776, the entire country was united. Within just a few decades that all changed. What caused this fight? Slavery.

The people living in the North had smaller farms that used free *labor,* or work. These states invested their money in banks and insurance. They built better transportation systems and worked hard at improving communication.

The people living in the South had *plantations,* or much larger farms. They grew crops like cotton and tobacco. They needed many more workers and invested much of their money in slaves.

The North and the South did not agree when it came to slavery. They fought every time a new state was added to the United States. The South did not want to give up slavery because that is how it made most of its money. The North did not feel slavery was right.

This map from 1860 shows how the states were divided. This division of states led to the Civil War. The map was printed from a wood engraving.

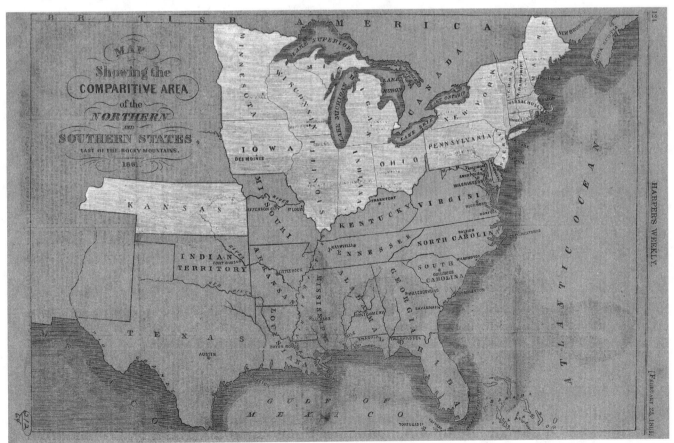

Library of Congress, LC-DIG-ppmsca-19483

North versus South

When the United States fought to gain its freedom from England in 1776, the entire country was united. Within just a few decades that all changed. What caused this fight? Slavery.

The people living in the North had smaller farms that used free *labor*, or work. These states invested their money in banks and insurance. They built better transportation systems and worked hard at improving communication.

The people living in the South had *plantations*, or much larger farms, that grew crops like cotton and tobacco. They needed many more workers and invested much of their money in slaves.

The North and the South disagreed when it came to slavery and fought every time a new state was added to the United States. The South did not want to give up slavery because that is how it made the majority of its money. The North felt that slavery was unfair.

This map from 1860 shows the division of the states. This division eventually led to the Civil War. The map was printed from a wood engraving.

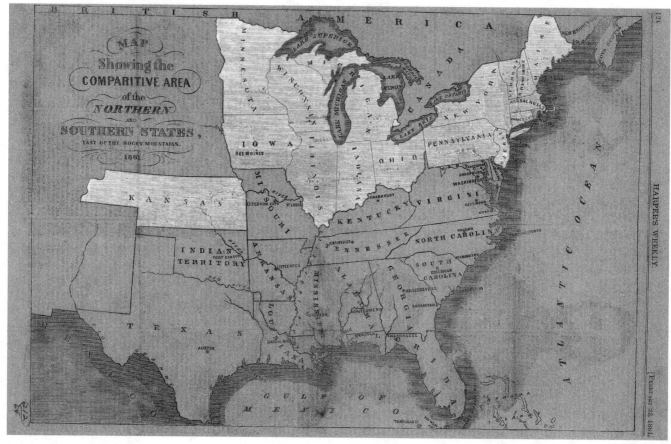

● ● ●   © Carson-Dellosa • CD-104863 • Evidence-Based Inquiry Using Primary Sources

North versus South

 Investigate

1. What did you notice first about the map? Why?

   _____

   _____

2. Which part of the map looks different from a map of the United States today? Why?

   _____

   _____

 Question

3. After studying this map, what do you want to learn more about?

   _____

   _____

4. How many states fought for the South in the Civil War? Which states? If you don't know, look in books and on safe Internet sites to find out.

   _____

   _____

💡 **Understand**

5. Based on this text, why do you think the South invested in slaves?

   _____

   _____

6. Why do you think the North invested in transportation and communication?

   _____

   _____

Take Your Money and Run

The American Civil War was fought from 1861 to 1865. The North was called the Union. The South was called the Confederacy. During these years, many people moved from the South to the North.

Some of those that moved were trying to get away from slavery. Many of them fought for the Union. Those that didn't sometimes had to live in *camps*. These were places to stay for the short term. They were not always the best places to live.

Others that moved were trying to get away from the South. Some did not agree with slavery. The South took land and money from people who did not agree with slavery. It also tried to force people to join its army. Many agreed with slavery. They just did not want to die in the war.

This photograph shows people leaving Virginia in 1862. They loaded everything they owned into their wagon and headed north. The original was a *stereograph*, a print showing the same picture side by side. When looked at in a stereoscope or with special glasses, it has a 3-D effect.

Take Your Money and Run

The American Civil War was fought from 1861 to 1865. The North was called the Union and the South was called the Confederacy. During these years, many people moved from the South to the North.

Some of those that moved were trying to escape slavery. Many of them fought for the Union. Those that didn't usually had to live in *contraband camps*. These were places to stay for the short term. They were not always the best places to live.

Others that moved were trying to escape the South. Some did not agree with the Confederacy. The South took land and money from people who did not agree with slavery. It also tried to force people to join its army. Many agreed with slavery but did not want to risk their lives in the war.

This photograph shows a family leaving Virginia in 1862. They loaded everything they owned into their wagon and headed north. The original was a *stereograph*, a print showing the same picture side by side. When looked at in a stereoscope or with special glasses, it has a 3-D effect.

Library of Congress, LC-USZ62-33104

Take Your Money and Run

The American Civil War was fought from 1861 to 1865. The North was called the Union and the South was called the Confederacy. During these years, many people moved from the South to the North.

Some of those that moved were African Americans trying to escape slavery. Many of them fought for the Union. Those that didn't usually had to live in *contraband camps*. These were places to stay for the short term. They were not always the best places to live.

Others that moved were white Americans trying to escape the South. Some did not agree with the Confederacy. The South took land and money from citizens who did not agree with slavery. It also tried to force people to join its army. Many agreed with slavery but did not want to risk their lives in the war.

This photograph shows a family escaping Virginia in 1862. They loaded everything they owned into their wagon and headed north. The original was a *stereograph*, a print showing the same picture side by side. When looked at in a stereoscope or with special glasses, it has a 3-D effect.

● ● ● © Carson-Dellosa • CD-104863 • Evidence-Based Inquiry Using Primary Sources

Take Your Money and Run

🔍 Investigate

1. What did you notice first about the photograph? Why?

   _____

   _____

2. What is happening in this photograph?

   _____

   _____

❓ Question

3. After studying this photograph, what do you want to learn more about?

   _____

   _____

4. What are some reasons people move today? If you don't know, look in books and on safe Internet sites to find out.

   _____

   _____

💡 Understand

5. Why is the title a good choice for this text and photograph?

   _____

   _____

6. Think about the way we pack and move today. Imagine packing and moving in 1862. How would it have been different?

   _____

   _____

Abram Lincoln?

In 1860, the men running for president of the United States printed many things. They did this to win votes. There were cartoons and sheet-music covers. Some men made pictures and banners. The banners were meant for parades.

Abraham Lincoln was running for president. His running mate was Hannibal Hamlin. The two men had never met. They belonged to the Republican Party. Lincoln and Hamlin did not get more than 50 percent of the vote. They won all of the North, however. This allowed them to win the election.

This red, white, and blue banner was printed on cloth, sometime around 1860. It was printed in color and had President Lincoln's name spelled wrong. Some people say that his name was shortened in order to fit on the banner. Others say that it was because not many people had heard of him when he decided to run for president. This is one mystery we may never know the truth about.

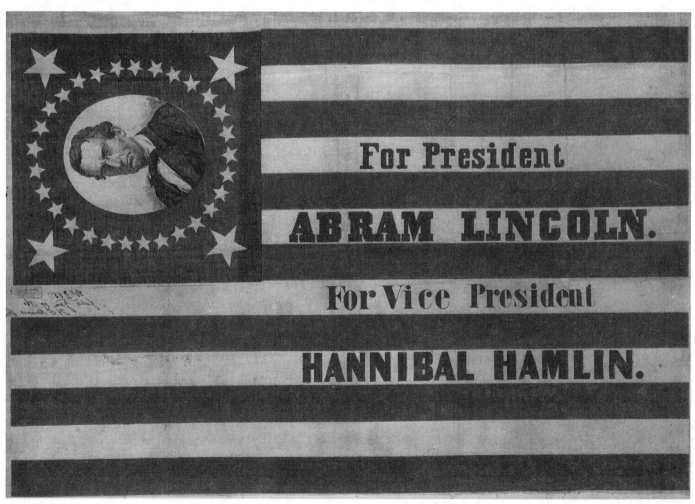

Library of Congress, LC-USZ62-14844

Abram Lincoln?

In 1860, the men running for president of the United States printed many things in order to try to win votes. They handed out cartoons, sheet-music covers, and pictures. They hung banners. The banners were hung in parades.

Abraham Lincoln was running for president with Hannibal Hamlin as his running mate. The two men had never met before the campaign. They belonged to the Republican Party. Lincoln and Hamlin got less than 50 percent of the vote in the election. They won all of the North, however. This allowed them to win the election.

This red, white, and blue banner was printed on cloth, sometime around 1860. It was printed in color and had President Lincoln's first name spelled as "Abram," not "Abraham." Some people say that his name was shortened in order to fit on the banner. Others say that it was because not many people had heard of him when he decided to run for president. This is one mystery we may never know the truth about.

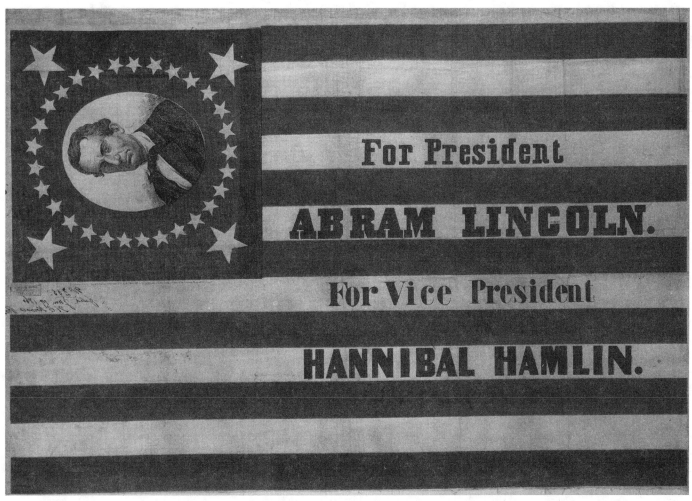

Library of Congress, LC-USZ62-14844

Abram Lincoln?

In 1860, the men running for president of the United States printed many things in order to try to win a presidential election. They handed out cartoons, sheet-music covers, and pictures. They printed large banners. The banners were hung in parades.

Abraham Lincoln was running for president and Hannibal Hamlin was running for vice president. The two men had never met before. They belonged to the Republican Party. Lincoln and Hamlin got less than 50 percent of the vote. They won all of the North, however, which allowed them to win the election.

This red, white, and blue banner was printed on cloth, sometime around 1860. It was printed in red, white, and blue. It spelled President Lincoln's first name incorrectly. Some people say that his name was shortened in order to make it fit on the banner. Others say that the mistake was made because few people had heard of him at the time he decided to run for president. This is one mystery we may never know the truth about.

Abram Lincoln?

 Investigate

1. What did you notice first about the banner? Why?

   _____

   _____

2. Why do you think the banner was designed in this way? How would you design it differently?

   _____

   _____

? **Question**

3. After studying this banner, what do you want to learn more about?

   _____

   _____

4. What do people running for president do today to try to get elected? If you don't know, look in books and on safe Internet sites to find out.

   _____

   _____

 Understand

5. Based on this text, why do you think Abraham Lincoln's name was spelled wrong?

   _____

   _____

6. This banner was made to look like a US flag. How is it different from the U.S. flag today? Why is there a difference?

   _____

   _____

A Voice for Peace

Almost one year after World War I began, over 1,200 women met in the Netherlands to speak for peace. They wanted the war to end. It was in April 1915. The meeting was called the International Congress of Women. Women came from all over the world. Many of those who went had worked long and hard to help women and children.

One woman, Jane Addams, was from the United States. She once went to England with a friend. She visited a house that helped the poor. She dreamed of opening one in the United States. Addams came home and worked very hard. She opened Hull House in 1889. It served many poor people living in Chicago. Her dream had become a reality!

Addams didn't stop after the Congress was ended. She kept working hard for those in need. She won the Nobel Peace Prize in 1931. The photograph shows Addams and others on the steamship *Noordam*. It was taken in 1915 and was printed from a glass plate negative.

     © Carson-Dellosa • CD-104863 • Evidence-Based Inquiry Using Primary Sources

A Voice for Peace

Almost one year after World War I began, over 1,200 women met in the Netherlands to speak for peace. They wanted the war to end. It was in April 1915. The meeting was called the International Congress of Women. The women came from countries all over the world. Many of those who went had worked long and hard to help women and children.

One woman, Jane Addams, was from the United States. She once traveled to England with a friend and saw a house that helped the poor. She dreamed of opening one in the United States. She came home and worked hard. She opened Hull House in 1889. It served many poor and immigrant people living in Chicago. Her dream had become a reality!

After going to the Congress of Women, Addams continued to work hard for those in need. She won the Nobel Peace Prize in 1931. The photograph shows Addams and others on the steamship *Noordam*. It was taken in 1915 and was printed from a glass plate negative.

Library of Congress, LC-DIG-ggbain-18848

A Voice for Peace

Almost one year after World War I began, over 1,200 women met in the Netherlands to speak for peace. It was in April 1915 and the meeting was called the International Congress of Women. The women came from countries all over the world. Many of those who attended had worked long and hard to help those in need, especially women and children.

One of those present, Jane Addams, was from the United States. She once traveled to England with a friend and saw a house that helped the poor. She dreamed of opening one in the United States. She came home and worked hard. She opened Hull House in 1889. It served many poor and immigrant people living in Chicago. Her dream had become a reality!

After traveling to the Congress of Women, Addams continued to work hard for those in need. She won the Nobel Peace Prize in 1931. This photograph shows Addams and others on the steamship *Noordam*. It was taken in 1915 and printed from a glass plate negative.

Library of Congress, LC-DIG-ggbain-18848

Name _____

A Voice for Peace

 Investigate

1. What did you notice first about the photograph? Why?

   _____

   _____

2. What is happening in this photograph?

   _____

   _____

 Question

3. After studying this photograph, what do you want to learn more about?

   _____

   _____

4. Is there an International Congress of Women still today? If not, do you think there should be? If you don't know, look in books and on safe Internet sites to find out.

   _____

   _____

 Understand

5. Based on this text and other information you have found, why do you think Jane Addams won the Nobel Peace Prize?

   _____

   _____

6. What topics might the women have discussed at the International Congress of Women? Create a meeting agenda that lists these topics.

   _____

   _____

Who Is Theodore Roosevelt?

Former US president Theodore Roosevelt was well known for his love of nature. However, as the print shows, there were many sides to him. He was born in 1858. His family called him "Teddy." He was very sick as a child. This meant he had to stay home for school. He loved animals and would study them.

President Roosevelt went to college and law school. He dropped out to become the youngest New York City representative. After his wife and mother died, he went out West. He became a cowboy and cattle rancher. Once he went back to New York, he held many public-service positions. He was a war hero from the Spanish-American War. He became the youngest US president in 1901. He won the Nobel Peace Prize in 1906.

After President Roosevelt's death in 1919, this print was made to honor his memory. It is called "And one man in his time plays many parts." Roosevelt truly had many "faces"!

Library of Congress, LC-USZ62-23052

Who Is Theodore Roosevelt?

Former US president Theodore Roosevelt was well known for his love of nature. However, as the print shows, there were many other sides to him. He was born in 1858 and his family called him "Teddy." He was very sick as a child so he stayed at home for school. He loved animals and liked to study them.

President Roosevelt went to Harvard College and law school. He dropped out to become the youngest New York City representative. After his wife and mother died, he went out West to become a cowboy and cattle rancher. Once he returned to New York, he held many public-service positions. He was a war hero from the Spanish-American War. He became the youngest US president in 1901. He won the Nobel Peace Prize in 1906.

After his death in 1919, this print was made to honor his memory. It is called "And one man in his time plays many parts." Roosevelt truly had many different "faces"!

Library of Congress, LC-USZ62-23052

Who Is Theodore Roosevelt?

Former US president Theodore Roosevelt was well known for his love of nature. However, as the print shows, there were many other sides to him. He was born in 1858 and his family nickname was "Teddy." He was very sick as a child and was homeschooled because of this. He loved animals and spent much time studying them.

He went to Harvard College and law school but dropped out to become the youngest New York City representative. After his wife and mother died, he went out West to become a cowboy and cattle rancher. Once he returned to New York, he held many public-service positions. He was a war hero from the Spanish-American War and became the youngest US president in 1901. He won the Nobel Peace Prize in 1906.

After his death in 1919, this print was made to honor his memory. It is called "And one man in his time plays many parts." Roosevelt truly had many different "faces"!

Library of Congress, LC-USZ62-23052

Name _____

Who Is Theodore Roosevelt?

 Investigate

1. What did you notice first about the print? Why?

_____

_____

2. What is happening in this print?

_____

_____

? **Question**

3. After studying this print, what do you want to learn more about?

_____

_____

4. Which other presidents especially loved nature? If you don't know, look in books and on safe Internet sites to find out.

_____

_____

 Understand

5. Look closely at the print. List the "parts" Roosevelt played in his lifetime.

_____

_____

6. Think about the many "parts" Roosevelt played. How do you think this helped him to be a better president?

_____

_____

Lady Liberty

People have been leaving their countries to move to the United States for over 200 years. Some move because of war. Others leave because they have no food. Many come for freedom. All of them think they will have better lives once they arrive in the United States.

Beginning in 1892, many of those arriving had to start at Ellis Island, New York. This is where the Statue of Liberty stands. Ellis Island was an immigration station until 1954. This meant that people had to check in there first.

Most of these people had been on boats for a long time. They would come into the harbor in New York and see "Lady Liberty." She meant freedom! France gave her as a gift to the United States in 1885. She could be considered an immigrant, too!

This print was made from a wood engraving. It shows people coming to the United States in 1887 and seeing the Statue of Liberty for the first time. They were on the deck of a steamer called the *Germanic*.

NEW YORK.—WELCOME TO THE LAND OF FREEDOM—AN OCEAN STEAMER PASSING THE STATUE OF LIBERTY: SCENE ON THE STEERAGE DECK.

Lady Liberty

People have been leaving their countries to move to the United States for well over 200 years. They leave for many reasons, including war, lack of food, and the promise of freedom somewhere else. All of them think they will have better lives once they arrive in the United States.

Beginning in 1892, many of those arriving had to start at Ellis Island, New York. This is where the Statue of Liberty stands. Ellis Island was an immigration station until 1954, which meant that people had to check in there first.

Most of the immigrants had been on boats for a long time. They would come into the harbor in New York and see "Lady Liberty." She meant freedom! France gave her as a gift to the United States in 1885. She could be considered an immigrant, too!

This print was made from a wood engraving. It shows people coming to the United States in 1887 and seeing the Statue of Liberty for the first time. They were on the deck of a steamer called the *Germanic*.

NEW YORK.—WELCOME TO THE LAND OF FREEDOM—AN OCEAN STEAMER PASSING THE STATUE OF LIBERTY: SCENE ON THE STEERAGE DECK.

Library of Congress, LC-USZ62-38214

Lady Liberty

People have been leaving their countries to immigrate to the United States for well over 200 years. They leave for many reasons, including war, lack of food, and the promise of freedom somewhere else. All of them believe they will have better lives once they arrive in the United States.

Beginning in 1892, many of those arriving had to start at Ellis Island, New York, which is where the Statue of Liberty resides. Ellis Island was an immigration station until 1954. This meant that people had to check in there first.

Most of the immigrants had been on boats for a long time. They would come into the harbor in New York and see "Lady Liberty." She meant freedom! France gave her as a gift to the United States in 1885, so she could be considered an immigrant also!

This wood engraving shows people coming to the United States in 1887 and seeing the Statue of Liberty for the first time. They were on the deck of a steamer called the *Germanic*.

NEW YORK.—WELCOME TO THE LAND OF FREEDOM—AN OCEAN STEAMER PASSING THE STATUE OF LIBERTY: SCENE ON THE STEERAGE DECK.

Name _____

Lady Liberty

 Investigate

1. What did you notice first about the engraving? Why?

   _____

   _____

2. What is happening in this engraving?

   _____

   _____

? Question

3. After studying this engraving, what do you want to learn more about?

   _____

   _____

4. What is Ellis Island used for today? If you don't know, look in books and on safe Internet sites to find out.

   _____

   _____

Understand

5. Based on the text and what you observe in the engraving, why do you think people were excited to see the Statue of Liberty?

   _____

   _____

6. Look closely at the engraving. Imagine you are a 10-year-old standing on the deck of the steamer boat. What are you thinking? How do you feel? In what ways will your life change?

   _____

   _____

A Hard Wall to Climb

For many years, people coming to the United States from other countries had to go through tests. This included medical and legal checks. If they passed, they could stay and work to become citizens. Some people worried that the new people would take their jobs.

In 1914, a group of people wrote the Burnett bill. It said that those coming into the United States should have to pass another test. This test had to do with reading and writing in English. They said that it would show if the immigrants would make good citizens.

Other people felt that this was not fair. Many people who moved to the United States were from southern and eastern Europe. They could not write or read in their native language or in English. There was no way for them to pass the test.

This cartoon is from 1916. It was written in response to the Burnett bill. It is titled "The Americanese Wall, as Congressman Burnett Would Build It." The subtitle says, "You're welcome in—if you can climb it!"

THE AMERICANESE WALL, AS CONGRESSMAN
BURNETT WOULD BUILD IT.
Uncle Sam: You're welcome in—if you can climb it!

Library of Congress, LC-USZ62-52584

A Hard Wall to Climb

For many years, people coming to the United States from other countries had to go through tests; these included medical and legal checks. If they passed, they could stay and work to become citizens. Some people worried that the new people would take their jobs.

In 1914, a group of people wrote the Burnett bill, which said that those arriving in the United States should have to pass another test. This one had to do with reading and writing in English. They said that it would show if the immigrants would make good citizens.

Other people felt that this was unfair. Many people who moved to the United States were from southern and eastern Europe. They could not write or read in their native language or in English. There was no way for them to pass the test.

This cartoon is from 1916. It was written in response to the Burnett bill. It is titled "The Americanese Wall, as Congressman Burnett Would Build It." The subtitle says, "You're welcome in—if you can climb it!"

THE AMERICANESE WALL, AS CONGRESSMAN
BURNETT WOULD BUILD IT.
UNCLE SAM: You're welcome in—if you can climb it!

Library of Congress, LC-USZ62-52584

A Hard Wall to Climb

For many years, people immigrating to the United States had to go through tests; these included medical and legal checks. If they passed, they could stay and work to become citizens. Some people worried that the immigrants would take their jobs.

In 1914, a group of people proposed the Burnett bill, which stated that those arriving in the United States should have to pass another test. This one had to do with literacy (reading and writing) in English. They said that it would show whether the immigrants would make good citizens.

Other people felt that this was unfair. Many people who immigrated were from southern and eastern Europe and could not read or write in their native language or in English. It would be impossible for them to pass the test.

This cartoon is from 1916. It was written in response to the Burnett bill. It is titled "The Americanese Wall, as Congressman Burnett Would Build It." The subtitle says, "You're welcome in—if you can climb it!"

THE AMERICANESE WALL, AS CONGRESSMAN BURNETT WOULD BUILD IT.
Uncle Sam: You're welcome in—if you can climb it!

Library of Congress, LC-USZ62-52584

A Hard Wall to Climb

 Investigate

1. What did you notice first about the cartoon? Why?

   _____

   _____

2. Study the drawing. Then, read the words beneath the drawing. It is meant to voice
   an opinion about the literacy test. What do you think the artist's opinion is?

   _____

   _____

? **Question**

3. After studying this cartoon, what do you want to learn more about?

   _____

   _____

4. What happened to the Burnett bill? Did it pass? If you don't know, look in books and
   on safe Internet sites to find out.

   _____

   _____

Understand

5. Based on this text, why do you think the Burnett bill was written? Do you think that this
   bill was fair? Why or why not?

   _____

   _____

6. Imagine leaving your country today and moving to Japan. As soon as you arrive you
   have to pass a Japanese reading and writing test in order to stay. Describe what that
   would be like for you.

   _____

   _____

Hard Work, Little Pay

People who moved to the United States from other countries had to find work. One job that they were usually able to find was working in the fields. Many farmers could not do all of the work on their farms themselves. Often, they hired immigrants to help out. They called them *migrant workers*.

Some might say that this was good, as the immigrants needed work. But there were many problems. Most of these jobs only lasted a short time. The workers often had nowhere to live but a small shed. Also, this was very hard work and they were outside all day. Finally, the workers made very little money. They might be paid $278 to $500 a year. This would be only $3,428 to $6,165 today. This was not enough money to provide for a family.

This photograph shows the Kastvan family working in a sugar beet field in Michigan in 1917. They traveled from New York City by train. This family is from Hungary. They are shown hoeing beets.

Library of Congress, LC-DIG-ncic-00689

Hard Work, Little Pay

People who moved to the United States from other countries had to find work. One job that they could find was working in the fields. Many farmers could not do all of the work on their farms themselves, so they needed to find help. Often they would hire immigrants. They called them *migrant workers*.

Some might say that this was good, as the immigrants needed work. But there were many problems. Most of these jobs only lasted a short time. The workers often had nowhere to live but small sheds. Also, this was very hard work and most of it was outside. Finally, the workers made very little money. They might be paid $278 to $500 per year, which would be only $3,428 to $6,165 today. This was not enough money to provide for a family.

This photograph shows the Kastvan family working in a sugar beet field in Michigan in 1917. They traveled from New York City by train. This family is from Hungary and is shown hoeing beets.

Library of Congress, LC-DIG-ncic-00689

Hard Work, Little Pay

People who immigrated to the United States from other countries had to find work. One job that they were able to find was working in the fields. Many farmers could not do all of the work on their farms themselves, so they hired people to help. Frequently, they hired immigrants. They called them *migrant workers*.

Some believed that this was good, as the immigrants needed work. However, there were many problems. The majority of these jobs only lasted a short time. Another issue was that many workers had nowhere to live but a small shed. Also, this was very hard work as they were outside doing physical labor all day long. Finally, the workers made very little money. They might be paid $278 to $500 per year, which would be only $3,428 to $6,165 today.

This photograph shows the Kastvan family hoeing beets in a sugar beet field in Michigan in 1917. They are from Hungary and traveled from New York City by train.

Library of Congress, LC-DIG-ncic-00689

Name _____

Hard Work, Little Pay

 Investigate

1. What did you notice first about the photograph? Why?

   _____

   _____

2. What is happening in this photograph?

   _____

   _____

 Question

3. After studying this photograph, what do you want to learn more about?

   _____

   _____

4. Are there still migrant workers in the United States? If so, what kinds of jobs are they doing? How often do they move around from place to place? If you don't know, look in books and on safe Internet sites to find out.

   _____

   _____

Understand

5. Based on this text and what you see in the photograph, why do you think immigrants worked on farms?

   _____

   _____

6. Imagine you are a child working in a beet field in Michigan in 1917. Describe how your life would be different.

   _____

   _____

Home on the Range

The US Congress passed the Homestead Act in 1862. This let any male over 21 years old claim 160 acres of land out west. In order for him to keep it, he had to build a house within six months. He also had to farm the land for five years.

Building a house was hard work. There were very few trees and stones on the prairie. One of the only materials available was *Nebraska marble,* or prairie sod. The strips of sod were very difficult to dig up. Building sod houses was extremely hard to do.

Living in a sod house was also hard. Settlers had to fight snakes, bugs, dirt, leaky roofs, and bad lighting. They had dirt floors and nothing was ever clean. On the plus side, the sod homes were cool in the summer and warm in the winter!

This photograph shows the Rawding family in front of their sod house. It was taken in Nebraska in 1886. The parents are shown with their four children, mules, dog, and their cow on the "roof!"

Library of Congress, LC-USZ62-8276

Home on the Range

The US Congress passed the Homestead Act in 1862. This allowed any male over 21 years of age to claim 160 acres of land on the prairie. In order for him to keep the land, he had to build a house within six months and farm the land for five years.

Building a house was hard work, especially since there were very few trees and stones on the prairie. One of the only materials available was *Nebraska marble*, or prairie sod. The strips of sod were very difficult to dig up. Building sod houses was extremely hard to do.

Living in a sod house was also hard. Settlers had to fight snakes, bugs, dirt, leaky roofs, and bad lighting. They had dirt floors and nothing was ever clean. On the plus side, the sod homes were cool in the summer and warm in the winter!

This photograph shows the Rawding family in front of their sod house. It was taken in Nebraska in 1886. The parents are shown with their four children, mules, dog, and their cow on the "roof!"

Library of Congress, LC-USZ62-8276

Home on the Range

The US Congress passed the Homestead Act in 1862, which allowed any male over 21 years of age to claim 160 acres of land on the prairie. In order for him to keep the land, he had to build a house within six months and farm the land for five years.

Building a house was hard work, especially since there were very few trees and stones on the prairie. One of the only materials available was *Nebraska marble,* or prairie sod. The strips of sod were very difficult to dig up, which made building sod houses extremely hard to do.

Living in a sod house was also hard. Settlers had to fight snakes, bugs, dirt, leaky roofs, and bad lighting. They had dirt floors and nothing was ever clean. On the plus side, the sod homes were cool in the summer and warm in the winter!

This photograph shows the Rawding family in front of their sod house in Nebraska in 1886. The parents are shown with their four children, mules, dog, and their cow on the "roof!"

Home on the Range

🔍 Investigate

1. What did you notice first about the photograph? Why?

    _____

    _____

2. What is happening in this photograph?

    _____

    _____

❓ Question

3. After studying this photograph, what do you want to learn more about?

    _____

    _____

4. Look closely at the photograph. What natural resources did the Rawding family use to make their sod house?

    _____

    _____

💡 Understand

5. People settled in many parts of the country as they moved west. What other natural resources could be used when building houses on the frontier? If you don't know, look in books and on safe Internet sites to find out.

    _____

    _____

6. Imagine living in a sod house on the prairie. Describe how your life would be different from what it is today.

    _____

    _____

Into the Wild

Daniel Boone was born in 1734 in Pennsylvania. His mother taught him to read and write. His father taught him how to live in the wilderness. He was only 12 years old when he got a rifle.

Daniel loved the outdoors and left home to serve during the French and Indian War. When his group was attacked, he escaped on a horse.

Later, he lived in North Carolina with his wife. He missed exploring the outdoors. He began leading expeditions to the West. In 1769, he helped discover the Cumberland Gap. This trail allowed settlers to reach the West.

He and his wife moved to Kentucky to begin a settlement. Many people moved with them. He had problems with the American Indians there, so they had to leave.

The photograph shows the cabin he lived in with his wife and children in Kentucky. It was taken in 1907, long after the Boone family lived there. The photograph was made from a glass plate negative.

Into the Wild

Daniel Boone was born in 1734 in Pennsylvania. His mother taught him to read and write, and his father taught him how to live in the wilderness. He was only 12 years old when he got a rifle.

Daniel loved the wilderness and left home to serve during the French and Indian War. When his group was attacked, he escaped on a horse.

He lived in North Carolina with his wife. He missed exploring the outdoors, so he began leading expeditions to the West. In 1769, he helped discover the Cumberland Gap, a trail that allowed settlers to reach the West.

He and his wife moved to Kentucky to begin a settlement. Many people moved with them. He had lots of issues with the American Indians there, so they had to leave.

The photograph shows the cabin he lived in with his wife and children in Kentucky. It was taken in 1907, long after the family lived there. The photograph was made from a glass plate negative.

Library of Congress, LC-DIG-det-4a13857

Into the Wild

Daniel Boone was born in 1734 in Pennsylvania. His mother taught him to read and write, and his father taught him how to survive in the wilderness. He was only 12 years old when he received a rifle.

Daniel loved the wilderness and left home to serve during the French and Indian War. When his expedition was attacked, he escaped on a horse.

He lived in North Carolina with his wife. He missed exploring the outdoors, so he began leading expeditions to the West. In 1769, he helped discover the Cumberland Gap, a trail that allowed settlers to reach the frontier.

He and his wife relocated to Kentucky to begin a settlement called Boonesboro. Many people moved with them. He had lots of issues with the American Indians there, so they had to leave.

The photograph shows the cabin he lived in with his wife and children in Kentucky. It was taken in 1907. The photograph was made from a glass plate negative.

Name _____

Into the Wild

 Investigate

1. What did you notice first about the photograph? Why?

    _____

    _____

2. What is happening in this photograph?

    _____

    _____

? Question

3. After studying this photograph, what do you want to learn more about?

    _____

    _____

4. The photographer used a glass plate to take the photograph of Mr. Boone's cabin. How did that work? How is it different from the materials photographers use today? If you don't know, look in books and on safe Internet sites to find out.

    _____

    _____

Understand

5. What materials did Daniel Boone use to make his cabin? Where do you think he got the materials?

    _____

    _____

6. Imagine you are exploring the frontier 200 years ago. Describe how your life would be different.

    _____

    _____

A Hopi Home

The Hopi tribe has lived in Arizona for thousands of years. Some say they were the first American Indians to live in what is now the United States. The word *Hopi* means hopeful or peaceful people. This truly describes the tribe. They do not usually take part in any wars. They work together as a tribe to meet the needs of everyone.

Hopi children are not named at birth. The tribe waits until the child is 20 days old. The parents will then hold the child up so that he faces the sun. They wait for the sun to "land" on the child. Then, a name is chosen.

Families live together in *adobe* houses. The houses are made of dried clay and stone. The houses have many levels. A ladder is used to go between the levels. As more people are born into the family, extra rooms are built.

The photograph was taken around 1921 and shows a pueblo home in Walpi, Arizona. Many of the homes in Walpi still look like this.

An old Hopi house, Walpi, Ariz.
Photo © 1920 Bushell

A Hopi Home

The Hopi tribe has lived in Arizona for thousands of years. Some say they were the first American Indians to live in what is now the United States. The word *Hopi* means hopeful or peaceful people. This truly describes the tribe. They do not usually participate in any wars. They work together as a tribe to meet the needs of everyone.

Hopi children are not named at birth. The tribe waits until the child is 20 days old. The parents will then hold the child up so that he faces the sun. After the sun "lands" on the child, a name is chosen.

Families live together in *adobe* houses. The houses are made of dried clay and stone. The houses have many levels and a ladder is used to go between the levels. As more people are born into the family, extra rooms are built.

The photograph was taken around 1921 and shows a pueblo home in Walpi, Arizona. Many of the homes in Walpi still look like this.

Library of Congress, LC-USZ62-102176

A Hopi Home

The Hopi tribe has lived in Arizona for thousands of years. Some say they were the first American Indians to live in what is now the United States. The word *Hopi* means hopeful or peaceful people and this truly describes the tribe. They do not typically participate in any wars. They work together as a tribe to meet the needs of everyone.

Hopi children are not named at birth. The tribe waits until the child is 20 days old and then the parents hold the child up so that he is facing the sun. After the sun "lands" on the child, a name is selected.

Families live together in *adobe* houses that are made of dried clay and stone. The houses have many levels and a ladder is used to travel between the levels. As more people are born into the family, extra rooms are built.

The photograph was taken in 1921 and shows a pueblo home in Walpi, Arizona. Many of the homes in Walpi still look like this.

An old Hopi house, Walpi, Ariz.
Photo © 1920 Dorkell

Library of Congress, LC-USZ62-102176

Name _____

A Hopi Home

 Investigate

1. What did you notice first about the photograph? Why?

   _____

   _____

2. What is happening in this photograph?

   _____

   _____

? Question

3. After studying this photograph, what do you want to learn more about?

   _____

   _____

4. Do any Hopi people live in the United States today? If so, do they still live in adobe homes? If you don't know, look in books and on safe Internet sites to find out.

   _____

   _____

Understand

5. Based on this photograph, what building materials did the Hopi use to create their homes? Why do you think they used these materials?

   _____

   _____

6. Imagine living in an adobe house. Describe how your life would be different.

   _____

   _____

Answer Key

Page 7

1. Answers will vary but should point out details from the photograph. 2. Answers will vary. 3. Answers will vary. 4. various countries, including Ethiopia, Pakistan, and more. 5. Answers will vary but should include an opinion. 6. Answers will vary but should show lifestyle differences between now and the early 1900s.

Page 11

1. Answers will vary but should point out details from the photograph. 2. Answers will vary. 3. Answers will vary. 4. Answers will vary but should include items sold by street vendors. 5. Answers will vary but should include an opinion. 6. Answers will vary but should show lifestyle differences between now and the early 1900s.

Page 15

1. Answers will vary but should point out details from the cartoon. 2. Answers will vary but should include jobs from today. 3. Answers will vary. 4. Vatican City. 5. Women are able to climb higher on the ladder since women's suffrage. 6. Answers will vary but should show lifestyle differences for women between now and the early 1900s.

Page 19

1. Answers will vary but should point out details from the ad. 2. Answers will vary but should show an understanding of slavery. 3. Answers will vary. 4. Yes, although no country admits it allows slavery. 5. Answers will vary but should include an opinion. 6. Answers will vary but should include an opinion and reasoning.

Page 23

1. Answers will vary but should point out details from the map. 2. Answers will vary but should mention states not formed at that time. 3. Answers will vary. 4. 11: Alabama, Florida, Georgia, Louisiana, Mississippi, South Carolina, Texas, Arkansas, North Carolina, Tennessee, and Virginia; 5. Answers will vary. 6. Answers will vary..

Page 27

1. Answers will vary but should point out details from the photograph. 2. Answers will vary. 3. Answers will vary. 4. Answers will vary. 5. Answers will vary but should include evidence from the text and photographs. 6. Answers will vary but should show lifestyle differences between now and the 1800s.

Page 31

1. Answers will vary but should point out details from the banner. 2. Answers will vary. Check drawings for creativity. 3. Answers will vary. 4. Answers will vary. 5. Answers will vary but should include an opinion. 6. Answers will vary but should show differences and reasons.

Page 35

1. Answers will vary but should point out details from the

photograph. 2. Answers will vary. 3. Answers will vary. 4. No. Answers will vary. 5. Answers will vary but should include an opinion. 6. Answers will vary but meeting agendas should show an understanding of women's issues at that time.

Page 39

1. Answers will vary but should point out details from the print. 2. Answers will vary. 3. Answers will vary. 4. Franklin D. Roosevelt, Lyndon B. Johnson, and Jimmy Carter; 5. Answers will vary but should include the many roles shown. 6. Answers will vary but should include an opinion.

Page 43

1. Answers will vary but should point out details from the engraving. 2. Answers will vary. 3. Answers will vary. 4. It is a national park. 5. Answers will vary but should include an opinion. 6. Answers will vary but should include personal connections.

Page 47

1. Answers will vary but should point out details from the cartoon. 2. Answers will vary. 3. Answers will vary. 4. No. 5. Answers will vary but should include an opinion. 6. Answers will vary but should include personal details.

Page 51

1. Answers will vary but should point out details from the photograph. 2. Answers will vary. 3. Answers will vary. 4. Yes, it was first vetoed by President Wilson but reenacted in 1917. Answers will vary based on research. 5. Answers will vary but should include details from the text and photograph. 6. Answers will vary but should include lifestyle differences.

Page 55

1. Answers will vary but should point out details from the photograph. 2. Answers will vary. 3. Answers will vary. 4. Answers will vary but should include sod, wood for windows and doors, and its placement into a hill. 5. wood, mud, adobe, shells, stone, straw, grasses, logs. 6. Answers will vary but should include personal details.

Page 59

1. Answers will vary but should point out details from the photograph. 2. Answers will vary. 3. Answers will vary. 4. Answers will vary but should show results of research and comparisons. 5. Wood from the forest and stones from the mountain. 6. Answers will vary but should include lifestyle differences.

Page 63

1. Answers will vary but should point out details from the photograph. 2. Answers will vary. 3. Answers will vary. 4. Yes. Many live in the same adobe homes as their ancestors. 5. mud and stone; They were available in the desert. 6. Answers will vary.